Wallpapering the Cat

Jan Dean lives near Manchester. She spends her time writing poems and stories in a cubby-hole under the stairs. When she's not writing she visits schools to perform her poems and run workshops. For fun she sings, runs a youth drama group, makes chocolate puddings and walks the dog – but not usually at the same time. She has a tall husband and two tall sons, so she is the shortest person in the house – but only on the outside. In an alternative reality she is six foot, thin and glamorous.

The Studio

Paint on the desks,
The walls and the floor,
Sometimes paint in the corridor,
Designs for duvets, ceramics and rugs,
Greetings cards, book covers, T-shirts and mugs,
Designs for this, designs for that,
We've enjoyed illustrating *Wallpapering the Cat*.

Yvonne Chambers and Maxwell Dorsey share a studio, near the Arsenal ground, with Sue, and Arnie the dog.

Also available from Macmillan

A Mean Fish Smile
poems by Jan Dean, Roger Stevens and Sue Cowling

I Did Not Eat the Goldfish
poems by Roger Stevens

Taking My Human for a Walk
poems chosen by Roger Stevens

The Colour of My Dreams
Poems by Peter Dixon

Wallpapering the Cat

Poems by
Jan Dean

Illustrated by
Chambers and Dorsey

MACMILLAN CHILDREN'S BOOKS

First published 2003
by Macmillan Children's Books
a division of Macmillan Publishers Ltd
20 New Wharf Road, London N1 9RR
Basingstoke and Oxford
www.panmacmillan.com

Associated companies throughout the world

ISBN 0 330 39903 9

Text copyright © Jan Dean 2003
Illustrations copyright © Chambers and Dorsey 2003

3 5 7 9 8 6 4 2

A CIP catalogue record for this book is available from the British Library.

Printed by Mackays of Chatham plc, Chatham, Kent.

Contents

Gift

Flat, under the mat
Like a pressed violet
In a lady's book
There is a vole.
It's body curled like a flower
It's tail a thin, thin stem.
It is my gift to you
And you will hate it
Almost as much as I think it wonderful.
That's because you are stupid
And I am a cat.

Fraction

Three's no good
Because three is always two and one
And I am never in the two.

You are in the two –
In every two there's ever been
There's something in you that the others want.

I can see it,
Even though it doesn't have a name
It's a sort of *shine* that I might share beside a two

But I'm the third one
In the three.

Dog Dreaming

Lying on the rug and dozing
– Rabbit dreams
Supposing that I'm nosing
Into burrows on the high hill,
Up above the furrows
On the black ploughed fields.
There's a wolf in me
And all the cunning of the pack
Runs in my blood
And rises in the hair along my back.

Lying on the rug and dozing
– closing half an eye . . .
Returning with a shuddering sigh
To the wild woods – wild ways,
Old, old days before you drew us in
And tamed us, claimed us,
Collared us and named us.
Gave us everything we wanted
Took from us everything we had.
Only now, in deep, deep sleep
My heart remembers how it was
And hunts.

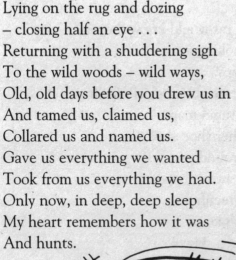

The Gardener's Daughter

I hated those glass slippers –
Where you could see my toes
Squashed like small white sausages
In clingfilm. I hated those glass slippers –
When I danced they steamed up.
'Ooo, sweaty feet!' the prince said
And I felt like a fool. That's why I ran,
Then the clock struck and I panicked –
Slipping in those stupid slippery slippers;
Sliding on the damp stone steps.
No wonder I lost one.
And I was late home.
Whoever thought a rat would know the way
Wants their head looking at.
Rats do not read maps.
Neither do princes care about a girl's feelings.
I never liked him. Stupid man –
Choosing a wife by her shoe size!
So when he came around
Touting that awful, awful slipper
I stayed put in the greenhouse
Tending my father's plants.
And when the kitchen skivvy
Tried it on, and up the shout went –

Yes! The slipper fits! – I kept my head down.
Let her have the husband, I thought,
I'll stick to my chrysanthemums.

Oh, Am I Still Here?

Oh, am I still here?
I thought that I was up.
I thought I was
      doing the dishes
      ironing the budgie
      and wallpapering the cat.
What me – *skiving*?
Reading when I should be up and at?
Now would I do a thing like that?

Oh, am I still here?
I thought that I was hard at work
    planting the baby
    hoovering a raspberry jelly
    taking next door's curtains for a walk . . .
I know that there are THINGS TO DO.
And I must deal with SERIOUS STUFF,

    But somehow, nothing's serious enough
To drag me out of this great story that I'm in.
So you can stand there and complain
As loud and crazy as you like.
Go on – if it makes you feel good – rant and shout.
BUT I'M INSIDE THIS BOOK AND I'M NOT
  COMING OUT!

It's Not What I'm Used To

I don't want to go to Juniors . . .

The chairs are too big
I like my chair small, so I fit
Exactly
And my knees go
Just so
Under the table.

And that's another thing –
The tables are too big.
I like my table to be
Right
For me
So my workbook opens
Properly.
And my pencil lies in the space at the top
The way my thin cat stretches into a long line
On the hearth at home.

Pencils – there's another thing.
Another problem.
Up in Juniors they use pens and ink.
I shall really have to think

About ink.

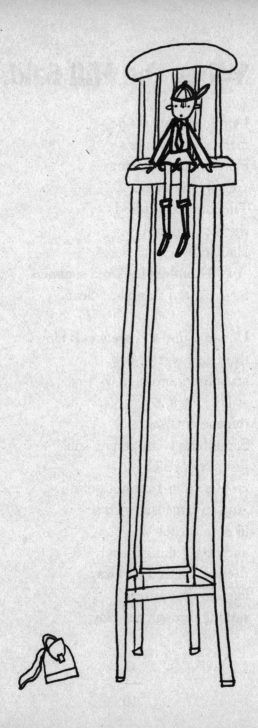

What the Hill Said

I am forgetting magic,
memories of wizards
blue fire and lightning
are slipping away.
The rain has washed
the rock smooth.
Hail and snow
And a hundred hundred summers
have blasted this place clean.

Underground strange winds blow
through caves
and phosphorous glows
as if . . . as if . . .
the currents say.
Something is happening still
just out of reach
an echo that I cannot quite . . .
And so forgetting grows
like stalactites
and magic sinks deeper
deeper. Far and far away
like old flint arrows
sinking through the clay.

Aaaaargh!

My aunty folds my face up,
Squeezes it like a concertina
Between her bony hands.
Then puckers up her mouth
into a wet doughnut –
Comeherecomeherecomehere
She says. Though I'm already there
And I can't get away.
Comeherecomeherecomehere
And I see it –
A slow-mo doughnut moving
Unstoppable through the air.
And I know, I just know,
That when it lands,
This killer kiss
Will be A WET ONE.

Davy Bones

Davy Bones lives in the wood
He rattles in the wind,
His ribs knock-knock
Like a chopping block
And his eye-holes whistle and sing.

Davy Bones will get me
I know he lies in wait,
I hear his rusty laughter
In the hinges of the gate.
Davy Bones will catch me
His smile is sharp and thin
And every time I close my eyes
The darkness fills with him.

Davy Bones is coming
On the stones his footsteps ring
His ribs knock-knock
Like a chopping block
And his eye-holes whistle and sing . . .

Grandma

Grandma is teaching the trees to sing,
She's building them giant harps –
Stringing their branches with long humming wires
And painting their limbs with pictures of larks.

Grandma is teaching the cows to dance –
Sewing them evening gowns,
Sprinkling sequins along their black tails,
Waltzing them over the downs.

Grandma is showing the frogs how to fly
High on the circus trapeze.
She swoops to the music of wild violins
Then gracefully hangs by her knees.

Girl in the Library

Pores over star maps
Like a sailor;
Behind her great iron pillars
Twist like barley sugar
To the pitched white roof
That keeps her from the sky.
Before her the staircase
Corkscrews into ground
She cannot leave.
She leafs longingly through galaxy and
       galaxy
While solid stones of all around
Slur and diffuse – unfold like petals
Or slow milk clouds in tea.
The library is melting as she reads,
Like time-lapse film of rainstorms
       clustering / blossoming
       clustering / blossoming
Space and space and million-studded space.

Horror

At the bottom of the cellar stairs
It was suddenly not all right.
Sent for Corona from the wooden crate
I stopped. Up in the shop my father served
Another customer and waited for the
    lemonade.

I saw the cheeses, huge and white as moons,
I saw the stacks of cans and barrelled lard,
The grating where the daylight leaked
    through ferns
And there they were. Two long pale frogs.
    Glistening.
Jewels on the dark stone flags. Tender,
    waxy,
Not emerald or malachite, but something
    sudden,
Clammy and alive with unexpected
    flutterings of skin.

And were there more of them? I felt the
    dread
Rise in me and was afraid to tread another
    step.
Underneath the darkness at my feet the stone
Could suddenly be soft as yogurt.

I did not want to hurt them.
In my heart I saw them dead.
Heard the sickly split of seaweed bladders
  bursting in my head.

'They won't hurt you. See?' my mother stroked
Their backs to make them hop, but I was frozen.
Their slithery spring, their shocking length
  of legs
Appalled me. Their rawness terrified me, I feared
The crunch of shell-like bone, the awful
  stickiness of eggs.

Grandad in the Garden

My grandad talks to radishes
He whispers to the ground
Telling them hot red secrets
So they grow plump and round.

My grandad sings to the lettuces,
Songs for their green hearts,
Watery salad music
For their tender leafy parts.

My grandad tells tomatoes
Squishy red-nosed jokes.
He whistles sea-shanties to curly kale
And tickles artichokes.

You may think my grandad's bonkers.
Crazy. Cracking up.
But every year his garden wins
The Blooming Best Gold Cup!

Midnight

Sleep is another country
We visit in our head.
I watch my brother sleeping now –
His eyelids heavy-smooth as lead . . .
A million miles away from me
Across our bedroom, in his bed.

It feels as if there's only me,
I'm the last boy left alive,
After the end of everything –
The last one to survive . . .
The screech owl cries, the wild wolf howls
The whole wide world's an ache.

For I am the last and lonely one
The only one left awake.

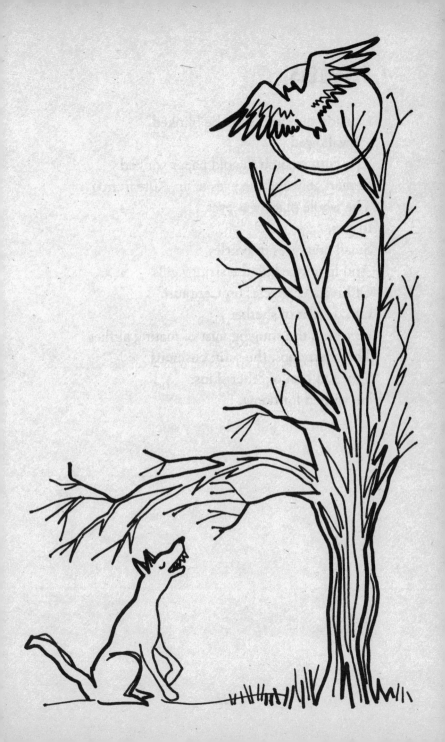

Meltis

Outside the sweetshop he blinked.
  Swallowed.
The butterscotch in gold paper winked
Remarkably like the eyes of an Antean frog.
The whole place was eyes
In jars,
Small creatures in bottles,
And liquorice like the stringy gills
Of his sister species on Centauri.
Oh, the fizz of sherbet
Fuzzed as the stinging mist of mating airflies
The cherry lips, the satin cushions
Spoke to him of other skins.
He wished for home.

Against the odds he took a box of
  Meltis Fruits
And watched them sugar sparkle
In the nest he made for them.
Thought of their liquid centres
Wet as eggs.
Blinked. Swallowed.
Turned on the bulb that hung above them.
Dreamed of their improbable
Desirable
Sweet
Sweet
Hatching.

Tent

In my tent
The light is orange.
And I sit here
Still
As if I'm set in jelly.

It's magic here
In this gold space
Where a minute stretches on . . .
   and on . . . and on . . .

Waiting For

This is the year of the moneybox
When Mrs Da Sylva will play
At holidays and new expensive frocks.
This is the year of the moneybox.
The unlocking year. The year of Paris
And Los Angeles and rubies big as rocks.
Oh, Mrs Da Sylva, cunning as the fox
And thrifty; careful of the last sweet scrape
    of jam,
Careful as the clever darning of worn socks,
Is taking a hammer to her moneybox.
Sick of saving, sick of prudent locks,
Dreaming of cruise ships waiting in the
    docks.
Mrs Da Sylva's time has come at last:
Box smithereened. Box withereened.
No more bacon boiled and butter-beaned.
For this is the year
            this is the year
            this is the year
                        of the moneybox.

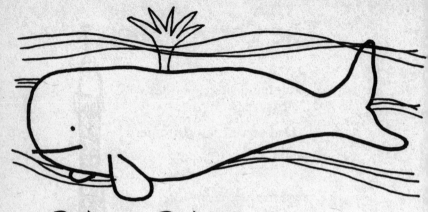

Beluga, Beluga

Beluga, beluga,
Your echoing song
Swoops through the waves
All the arctic-night long.
Beluga, beluga,
Strange white whale
Sings through the water
Ghostly and pale.

Beluga . . . Beluga . . .
Your name is a bell
Ringing where emerald icebergs dwell.
Ringing where secrets shine under snow,
Where silver fish shoal and ice-hurricanes blow.
Out of that green and icy sea
Beluga is spinning a dream for me . . .

The Corner Shop

Scotch hands in the butter
Pat   Pat   Pat
My Dad served the customers
Just like that.

Bacon in the slicer
Whiz   Zin   Zin
See the bacon slices
Thick   Thin   Thin.

Corona in big bottles
Pop   Pop   Pop
And tuppence for the empties
In our grocers shop.

Now food comes in packets –
Sliding down conveyor belts.
Or it comes out of a freezer –
Hurry home before it melts.

The supermarket's bigger
A food-palace . . . All the same
The lady on the checkout
Doesn't know your name.

Riding the Chair Lift

Stand still
Here on this high hill
And wait
While the man hooks and turns
The swinging chair.

Stand still
Until it creeps right up behind you
Then half-leap, half-hop
Hey-hup! Up!
Away into the air.

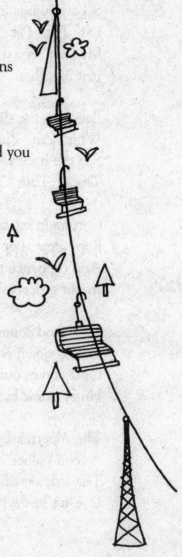

Below the earth shelves sharply
And suddenly we are sitting in the space of birdsong
Our shoes above the trees
Skimming above the sparrows.
Gliding to the quiet hum
Of wire and pulley. Slowly
Slowly now we come
Down over the wooded slopes
Where houses nestle in the trees
Like Lego bricks in broccoli.
The whole city is for dolls
And matchbox toys.
There's no noise, no bustle
Only the great calm of the forest
And the strange creak of the chair lift
As we drift like slow snow
Down
Down
Down.

Torches in the Wood

Torches in the wood –
All the trees are like bones
Tall and strange and skeleton thin . . .
The cold wind moans.

Torches in the wood –
The small yellow beams
Light the spooky branches
With tiny pinprick gleams.

Torches in the wood –
And hairy scary games
Ghostly owl-hoot voices
Calling out names.

Torches in the wood –
On a wild winter night.
Shivering with pleasure
At each delicious fright.

Mammoth Tasks, or – Why the Mammoth Became Extinct

Eat grass
Eat more grass
Rub tusks on tree trunk
Eat grass.

Make huge hairy trumpeting noise
With my lovely mammoth trunk –
Attract beautiful lady mammoth
Make mammoth music together,
Make baby mammoths,
So that mammoth kind will never vanish from the
    earth . . .
Later.

Right now
Eat grass.

Three Ways of Going into the Cold Sea

Tip toe
  Slip toe
  Dip toe in the water
  Shiver, scream and sigh

Step and breathe and stop
  Wade and hiss and hop
  Till the waves just over top you,
  Slosh and slap and slop you.

Hurtle down the shingle
  Charge and plunge and tingle
  In the gasping icy twinkle
  Of a wide wide eye.

In the Elephants' Graveyard

The stone angels have very big ears.
And blow their own trumpets.
If there are ghosts here
They float silently
Like huge grey moths
With only a sigh or a fluttery flap
Or a twinkle of tusk
To hint at their passing.
Their long slow passing
Grey in the grey light of dusk.

Sweets from Strangers

In the gingerbread house, the gingerbread mouse
Is nibbling away in the walls.
And the gingerbread witch, with liquorice pitch,
Is tarring the roof before the rain falls.

The sugar is sparkling. Each crystal and grain
Is as bright and as sharp as a pin.
Marshmallow cushions plum-pillow the chairs
And the open door whispers 'Come in . . .'
The lemonade's poured. The biscuits are baked.
The whole place is shimmering and fragrant with cake.

The candyfloss curtains, pretty and pink,
Sway in the honeydew air.
They look so lovely that no one would think
That anything bad could be there.
But don't trust your eyes. For the sugar tells lies
In that diamond glitter, hundreds of flies
Are trapped by the sticky sweet web in disguise.

Each day the witch picks them out with a pinch
Of her long scritch-scratch nails. Tweaks inch by inch
Of the ginger house clean,
So that never a one of those flies can be seen.
Not a hairy black leg.
Not a papery wing.

Not a bluebottle buzz. Not a hint. Not a thing.

She shines up the barley-twist butterscotch hall
And is always quite ready
Should somebody call . . .

Sleepwalking with Birds

They are there, I know they are there.
In the wardrobes, in the hidden places
Birds. Bright birds.
Dayglo orange, flame yellow, jungle green,
The turquoise of the seas of dreams.
And when I open up the cupboard doors
Out they fly – then follow
As I wind my way
Up through the house . . .
Opening every door . . .
More, more . . . a dazzle of feathers,
A rainbow of birds fluttering
Like gulls swooping to a rising net
Up, up. Until I stand high in the loft
and open the wide window
The cold night wakes me,
Sharp with icy stars.
While all around my dream birds fly
And melt, escaping to the high black sky.

The Unlucky Baker

I bake the bread for harvest –
White flour laced with arsenic
So nibbling mice that fringe
The surplices and cassocks die
And desiccate beside the heating ducts.
A neat trick taught me by a priest
Who hated cats.
He it was who gave the tainted rice
To shower about the shining brides.
Churchyard pigeons streak the headstones.
  Make mess.
And is not cold confetti ugly after rain?
He had me plug the air gaps in the organ loft
Then when our faulty gas pipes leaked
Bade me sweep the dead bats rustling in a
  heap.
I remember their soft fur, the rough hessian
  of the sack.
He didn't die of injuries sustained
When falling from a pulpit crumbling
With deathwatch beetle.

But he should have done.

Sheep Look White Until it Snows

In summer they are clouds on legs
White as mist
And light as candy floss
Dotting the high hill like cotton.
But now, in January sleet
They're grey and grizzled
Under winter's drizzled slushy rain.
After frost they're dreary, stained.
Against the flurries and the drifts
They're yellower than ancient paper;
The colour of a bonfire's clotted smoke.
But every summer they still fool me
Every summer when the sun is bright
I really do believe that sheep are white.

Out There

The minutes that disappeared last night
Between TV and the pillow fight;
The great idea that slipped away;
A dream turned misty at start of day
The chance to say what you wanted to say,
Before all that other stuff got in the way.
Everything lost finds its own true place
Down the back of the sofa in cyberspace.

Lost your temper? Or lost your thread?
Your heart, or your bottle? Your cool or your head?
You'll find them all tangled and mangled and strange,
All fuddled and muddled and de-rearranged –
For everything lost will find its place
Down the back of the sofa in cyberspace.

When you're lost in thought you'll feel the spin
Of that hungry black hole that's pulling you in,
With a spring-toothed sneer and a quicksand grin
And a smothering smile as sharp as a pin –
As you sink in that dark deep dangerous place
Down the back of the sofa in cyberspace.

A Mother's Confession
(or : What You Have Always Suspected ...)

As soon as you are asleep in bed
I unlock the secret cupboard
Where I keep all the chocolate
And I eat it and eat it and eat it.
I don't share it with anybody
And I don't give half a hoot about my teeth.

As soon as you are tucked all tidy in your bed
I put my feet up on the sofa – shoes still on,
Or if I take them off I don't undo the laces first,
Then I drink fizzy cans and eat crisps,
And practise blowing huge, round, pink bubbles
Out of Hubba-Bubba gum.

Once you're asleep
I watch *those* programmes on the telly
(The ones I always say are trash)
And I don't go to bed at a sensible time –
Even though I'm really, really tired.
I don't go because I'm a grown-up
And I can do what I like
And you can't stop me.
Ha. Ha. Ha.

Advice to the Horticulturalist

Sing into the trumpet of the amaryllis,
Read lists of numbers to the clematis,
Recite long poems to the patient cactus,
But whisper, whisper to the hyacinth.

Science fiction for the spider plant,
Victorian sermons for the pyracanth.
A hellebore will relish murder
Mock orange has a taste for Thurber.
Avoid polemic near delphiniums –
They get the blight from fixed opinions.
Invective will not put things right
If weeds are rioting.
Nor will abuse be any use –
They like the frisson, flourish on the spite.

A weeping willow fed on secrets
Grows and grows and grows.
While golden rod and Russian vine
Enjoy experimental prose.
Forget-me-nots spread fast as gossip,
Don't tell a lily lies,
You can be risqué with a tulip,
A rose will thrive on sighs.

So sing into the trumpet of the amaryllis,
Spout logarithms to the clematis,
Recite your epic to the patient cactus,
But whisper, whisper to the hyacinth.

What's the Point of This?

You're right!
It is a waste of time
There is no point in doing all this stuff
So we won't watch this film about the Romans,
Or make a model of Vesuvius
We'll do something that you'll need
in REAL LIFE.
We'll practise *queuing* . . .
No no! Not like that –
You're much too much spread out.
Squash up! Let's stand together
Shoulder to shoulder like on trains and tubes.
Oh good – it's raining – now we can go outside
And practise waiting for the number 36
Craig – go fetch a bucket and then dip it in that puddle
    there
I think I'd like to simulate the lorries passing by.
We'll cut out break – the real world carries on
Oblivious – and so shall we.
You are not yet grown-ups, not yet quite 'free'
Regard this as a little taste of sweet reality.

Who's There?

Nobody breaks the windows,
Nobody spills the milk.
Nobody creeps round the house at night
As silent and secret as smooth black silk.
Nobody digs deep holes in the garden,
Nobody scratches long scars in the wall.
I am afraid of Nobody.
When I'm alone will Nobody call?

Nobody whispers scary stories
To frighten the little ones tucked in their beds.
Nobody growls and makes wicked noises
To make them pull covers over their heads.
When there's just me by myself, I will shudder.
Hush myself. Still myself. Shiver with fear,
Because, in the shadows, I know who is waiting –
Watchful and hungry – Nobody's here . . .

Reading in the Attic

At the top of the house
You can hear the feathered mutter
Of pigeons on the roof,
Or the gurgle of the gutter,
And the light shines yellow
Through the blinds like butter.

In this soft-sound space
In this gentle, golden air
I breathe the papery smell of books
And suddenly the 'where'
Of where I am dissolves
And I'm not here – I'm *there* . . .

Where time and space are folded
In the pages of a book,
And to travel anywhere or when
I only have to look
Then be reeled in like a fish
On a shining story-hook.

The Barber-Surgeon at Avebury

I am here
in the third blade of grass from the left,
and here in the trip-you-up tree root.
Some of me
lurks in yellow lichen.

It isn't what I meant.
I meant to die
insignificant
in my own bed,
in my own house,

                    – the kitchen smelling
                    of iron pans and mackerel
                    the bedrooms of elderflowers –

but everyone knew
the stones
were the work of the devil.
It was duty, you see,
dragged me into this.

                    We went out righteous;
                    spades and psalms
                    would do it.

Each of us took turns
to dig the pit.
I blistered – more used to scissors
than a spade
'Look,' I said
and spread my hand into the sun
that warmed the ready grave.
The women laughed,
said I was soft as leeches,
that hard work never hurt a man.

The blacksmith lifted Catherine with one
    hand.

In the middle of the jokes
the sarsen fell

                – green sky
                green earth
                green stone
                the sapling by the ditch
                fat Catherine's laugh
                the crumbs of soil
                roll, rolling down
                the damp smell
                and the feel of dirt –

The boasting muscles froze.

> The stone was heavy
> Nothing for it but to leave me
> buried with the pagan.

In my own home,
in my own bed,
no one would have wondered.

I meant to die
        quietly, without fuss,
        to hear the click of beads
and be forgotten.

But I am here.
Pinned by the stone,
held in the grass.

Fast in memory
alive in eyes
that watch the lichen
on the yellow stone.

Footnote: In the past, stone circles were regarded by some people
as evil, so they were often destroyed or in the case of the stones at
Avebury, buried. Hundreds of years later they were dug up to reveal
a skeleton and a leather bag containing a barber-surgeon's tool.

Respect

I know the difference between fish and fingers
But do you know that I know?
I like the doubt that lingers in your mind
And makes you nervous round my tank at feeding time.
Sometimes I stare right through the glass
And into your wide eyes
I hear the nervous edgy sighs
I see the way you never quite completely turn your back
As if the pane between us might just crack . . .
Then in the gush and slither of escape
You'd meet *piranha* face to face
You alone and me alone
And tooth and tooth and tooth to bone.

Choosing

'He's nice. Oh, look at him!' – My mother's
  voice
About the baby boy whose red hair marked
  him out
From all the others in the line of cots.
The first part of my special story,
Told before I knew what words were.
Heard well. And over, over once again,
Whenever spots or fever tangled sleep
She'd tell about that boy who'd tempted her,
That red-haired boy, the one they almost had
Before they found the small fat baby,
  sleeping.
– Ah, and then she opened those big eyes
Big blue eyes just like Dad's, and laughed.
And 'That's the one,' he said. –
My story goes like that. They picked me,
Not that golden baby with the shining hair.
I know I'm loved.
Why is it then I buy, quite regularly,
Tubes of 'Chestnut Glow' or henna from the
  chemist's shop?

The Unit of Sleep

I measure fun in grandads –
The best slide in the park is three whole
  grandads long.

I measure ponds.in duckfuls –
This is a lake. Tons of ducks. Swans. Green
  mud, good pong.

Picnics are weighed in chocolate biscuits.
Don't care if they do melt, so long as there's
  a lot.

Holidays stretch in yards of sunshine.
Sand, seaslap, shingle. Donkey smell and
  leather. Hot.

Journeys are timed in songs and stories –
From here to Aunt Em's house the wicked
  witch schemes
And as we arrive there the Prince rescues
  Snow White.

The unit of sleep is dreams.

Shadow Places

It is quiet
In the shadow places.
Quiet
At the edges of things.

The air moves
In strange swirls,
As if invisible dancers
Turn and turn . . .

. . . In the quiet places,
The shadow places,
The grey ghost spaces
At the blurred edge of the world.

Nativity

When God decided to be bones and skin and blood like
　　us
He didn't choose a palace, nothing grand – no frills and
　　fuss.
He slipped in through the back door, with the straw
　　and hay and dust.
He just became a baby with no choice but to trust.
And love us without question, as every baby must.

But Creation knew the wonder of this tiny newborn
　　king.
The crystal depths of space were touched, the air itself
　　would sing.
The Word is flesh. The silence of the glittering stars is
　　shattered. Heaven rings.
The sky blazed wild with angels, whose song was fire
　　and snow.
When God lay in his mother's arms two thousand years
　　ago.

Three Slow Visitors

When Christmas is over
And New Year is past
We three slow visitors arrive at last.

Too late for the angels
We wonder and long
For the piercing white beauty of feathery songs.

We wandered the wastes
Where the wind and the sand
Whispered and shifted and remade the land.

And now by the Maker
Of all things we stand
Mysterious gifts in our trembling hands.

The gold and the incense
Are all fine and good
And the myrrh has its meaning too – all understood.

But here – at our mercy
Lies God – and we shiver
Just what is the gift here? And who is the giver?

The Rubber Plant Speaks

Mostly they ignore me,
The white plants who walk.
Or bring me water in their leaves.

I wonder how they feed?
With their stubby roots?
And is there green beneath their skins?

Sometimes they talk to me,
But never listen.
They do not recognize my voice.

No one hears. No one hears.
No, not even him,
The little orange plant that swims.

I Never Trusted Herod

With his bright beady eye
With his slippery pink smile
And his, 'See you bye and bye . . .'
I never trusted Herod,
So why, oh why,
Did I tell him what I knew
Of the star in the sky?
I never trusted Herod
With his hand on my arm
Promising he meant the best
Saying 'There's no harm . . .'
I never trusted Herod
But I blabbed just the same
Shot my mouth off, said too much
And so I feel to blame
For what happened – for the soldiers,
When finally they came . . .

I dream a lot of Herod
I dream we never met,
And all those little children
Are happy – living yet.
In my dreams the snow shines white.
The ice does not melt red
But when I wake I find
that still the dead are dead.

And the baby? Did he find him?
We left so fast – I never knew.
The baby underneath the star,
Did they kill him too?

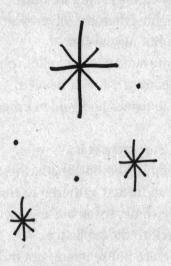

Angels

We are made from light.
Called into being we burn
brighter than the silver-white
Of hot magnesium.
More sudden than yellow phosphorus.
We are the fire of heaven;
Blue flames and golden ether.

We are from stars.
Spinning beyond the farthest galaxy
In an instant gathered to this point
We shine, speak our messages then go,
Back to the brilliance.
We are not separate, not individual,
We are what we are made of. Only
Shaped sometimes into tall-winged warriors,
Our faces solemn as swords,
Our voices of joy.

The skies are cold;
Suns do not warm us;
Fire does not burn itself.
Only once we touched you
And felt a human heat.
Once, in the brightness of the frost.
Above the hills, in glittering starlight,
Once, we sang.

Cat

My bones are rubber jelly
I leap, but never fall
I lie like a long fur collar
On the shoulders of the wall.
My eyes are ancient jewels
Like gems from Pharaoh's tomb
Even when you think I'm sleeping
I monitor the room.
My soul is grey and misty
Shadowy . . . secret . . . free . . .
I rise like smoke, escape and go
No one possesses me.

Canary

The dome of his head
Is round as an egg.
His skull as delicate as shell,
The bones inside his little body
Fine as pins.

I can spread his yellow wings
Like feather fans,
But he won't sing,
Not again. Not ever.
He is light as dust
And I must bury him.

His bright body
Like sunshine in a box
Deep in the shade
Of dark rhododendrons.
Muffled. Silent.
In the soft black soil.

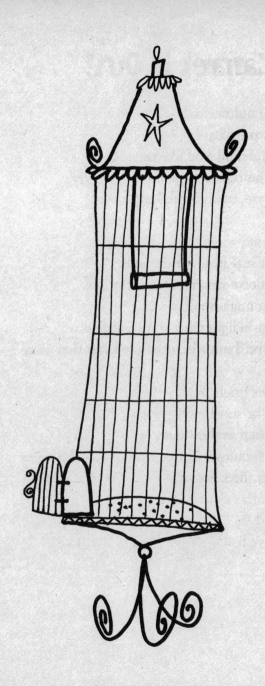

Their Secret is Out!

Teachers are not normal.
Anybody knows that –
Only they pretend to be like us
By shopping in the supermarket
And buying jam and cornflakes.
It's a con.
They don't eat.
They are not real inside their bodies –
They are full of wires and micro-circuits.
They feed on mathematics
And spellings like *psoriasis* and *bouillabaisse*.
Do not believe them when they tell you they were
young
   once.
It is a lie.
The factory that makes them
Does not do 'young'.
It only makes three sorts:
Bat-eared,
Needle-nosed,
And Eagle-eyed.

Banned

Mud's good.
But it's banned.
Because we tread in it, and then we tread it in.

The field's good.
But it's banned.
We're not allowed in the field unless it's dry,
Which it never is.

Snow's good.
But it's banned.
Because it melts and goes to slush
And then the dirt and slush gets mushed
And makes mud.

Mud's good.
But it's banned.

Taking Care

There's a dungeon underneath our school
Where the caretaker keeps prisoners.
You hear them moaning when the wind
Hoots round the downspouts.
And echoes from the drains.
There are howls
And chains clank.
There's a dungeon underneath our school
Where the caretaker takes care
Of everyone who's messed up on his floor
Or left chairs somewhere where a chair's no right to be.
I don't sleep easy any more –
Not since the handle of the PE cupboard door
Came right off in my hand.
Not since the incident with pancake batter
– It wasn't me, but nobody believes . . .
I don't sleep well.
At playtime I don't stray from the group.
He watches me.
I hold my breath when Miss sends us on messages.
Not me. Not me.
He'll get me one day,
On the corridor. Alone.
And then I'll go down one of those dark passages.

Temptation

He'll never miss just one . . .
So I took it.
Then I lifted up the box and shook it.
Seemed as heavy.
Sounded just as full.
All next day I felt that chocolate pull . . .

He'll never miss just one . . .
So I nicked it.
He'd never, never tell that I had picked it
Peeled the wrapper off and flicked it
Shiny in the bedroom bin.
All next day I knew the chocolate would win

A week on – and he's noticed.
Now he's twigged the box is light
And soon there'll be one big-time fight.
He'll guess who did it – and guess right.
For one and one and one and one
Kept adding on and on and on . . .
My last chance – like the chocolate's – gone.

It's a Long Way Down

It's a long way
         down.
Ooo, it's a long way
         down.
As the wind whistles
         past me
Weee oooo eeee . . .
         I can see –
         It's a long
                  way
                  down.

I'm walking the pipe
high over the stream
that bridges the banks
from green to green
the thick black pipe
that runs between
dizzy like being in a horrible dream
and I want to turn back
and I feel the scream
stuck in my throat
like something I've swallowed
and I breathe like a dry fish.
My heart beats hollow.

It's a long way down.
Ooo, it's a long way down.
As the wind whistles past me
Weee oooo eeee . . .
        I can see –
        It's a long

                way
                down.

I'm walking the pipe
way up over the brook
I stare straight ahead
I daren't even look
at my feet, as my toes try to grip
through the soles of my shoes,
try to hold to the metal
that's smooth as smooth
I'm out in the middle now
and I can't move . . .
It's a long way down.
Ooo, it's a long way down.
As the wind whistles past me
Weee oooo eeee . . .
        I can see –
        It's a long

                way
                down.

Olympic Diver

After the long straight climb I walk the
       plank.
It should sing – taut and tender as the
       wounded string
Of a violin. Still and high. I stand.
Breathe.
It is time for transformation.
I gather myself – feet curl to talons,
Calves, thighs muscled like a bird's to the
       spring,
I fly. Up and out into the above.
Shift into a coil. Spin, straighten, fold and
       open,
Serpent to arrow entering the plummet.
I am molten, a tear of dropping lead.
I fall and water opens for me. No splash.
We are the same – water to water.
I eel in a line of silver. Broken bubbles
Scatter, run with me.
And then the gathering again.
Flick.
I am in air. Still
beside the still green square. Listen.
In the silence is triumph.
The gentle ebb is proof of magic.
All is as it was.

The Last Word

is beer
Well, *zythum*, which is Ancient Egyptian beer.

Almost the last word
        is *zugzwang*,
which is a seriously clever *gotcha* move in chess.
Though I suppose you could zugzwang anyone
or anything if you were smart enough.
        – Sorry, Mum, I can't tidy my room just now
        because I have to do my homework
        which is watching the adverts on TV –
Now that's zugzwang.

Then there's *zucchini*
        A kind of courgette.
Mum stands over me till I eat mine.
When it's zucchini I'm totally zugzwanged.
I'd rather be a zonked zombie than a zugzwanged
    zucchini eater
But then, you can't win 'em all.

Spell for Getting Rid of a Fed-up Mood

Whisper the story of the three little pigs in a bottle
Then screw the lid up tight.
Take the bottle up a hill.
At the top shout *PIG BOTTLE!*

Take the bottle through a wood.
In the middle of the thickest thicket
Whisper *wolf bottle . . .*

Then take the bottle to the river/the sea/a bucket in
the back garden
And drop it in the water.
Then close your eyes and watch
The journey . . .

       Tossed about in storms
       The bottle bobs
       And inside all the pigs are jiggled
       And the wolf gets seasick
       Until suddenly
       On rocks/sand/shingle
       The bottle's breached –
       Or smashed against the shore
       And the story runs out . . .

Can you see it?
Can you?
When you can the spell begins to work . . .

An Owl Flew in my Bedroom Once

My attic bedroom had two windows –
One that opened high above the street
And a skylight – a tile of thick glass
Like a see-through slate.
And through it fell the moonlight
Coring the darkness like an apple-peeler.
Suddenly in that long cylinder of light
Appeared the owl, mysterious and grey
In that cold moon.
He flew in silently – a piece of night adrift –
Escaped. He circled, didn't settle
On the banister or rail.
There was no rattle of his talons,
No gripe or stomp
To make him solid with their sound,
He simply floated in – turned wide – and floated out . . .
No down or limy dropping
Nothing to prove he'd ever been at all.

An owl flew in my bedroom once, I think.

The Stuntman's Diary

Monday   Fell from the roof of twenty storey building
Chips for tea.

Tuesday   Crashed motorbike
Escaped from burning car
Fired from cannon
Fed ducks.

Wednesday Swam through crocodile infested swamp
Wrestled python
Took guinea pig to vet's.

Thursday   Bungie jumped from Humber bridge
Got blasted in underground explosion
Washed hair.

Friday   Grounded
Mum threw wobbly – said my room was a
    disgrace
Said I had to clean the wardrobe top
And underneath the bed.
But I wouldn't.
Couldn't.
It just isn't fair.
How am I supposed to do that stuff
When there are *spiders* there?

Dear Mum

I am not happy here.
It's cold and wet and not like Syria at all.
If we can't see the distant hills – that means it's raining.
If we can see them clear – it means the rain's about to
   fall.

Dear Mum,
There's nothing here worth having.
We're civilizing brutish British jerks –
Handing out state-of-the-art technology,
Giving them hypocaust and baths – the works.

We've built some villas, laid some mosaic,
Straightened the winding roads, brought order here.
And in return I sneeze until my nose aches.
We've given up sweet wine for bitter beer.

Dear Mum,
The natives here are fearsome.
They paint their bodies blue – a waste of dye.
The icy wind blows round our knocking kneecaps,
We'll all be turning blue now by and by.

There are no chariot races. There's no circus.
No lions chomping Christians for a joke.
They underpay us and they overwork us,
It makes me want to spit. It makes me choke.

I wish that I was home. I'm off the Empire –
They can stick their army and their eagles too.
As soon as night falls and the rotten rain stops
I'm going to leg it home, dear Mum, to you.

Too Weird

The TV is leaking;
Yesterday a woman with a freeze-dried smile
did a dance routine with the Dyson
in our living room.
Slowly my brother is becoming a cartoon;
His new friends all have weird names
And when they leave at dusk
They fade into the dark
Like pencil sketches on grey paper.
And now there is *this*. This *frog*.

One minute it was in a jungle,
Suckered on a fronded leaf
Like gleaming jelly,
And then with one determined leap
It was here –
not enjoying the dry woolliness of the rug
not happy at all
On the baked bricks of the hearth.
Stuck, the wrong side of the screen.

Now I read the telly pages
In the paper –
    There's dinosaurs
    And tidal waves
    And aliens
    And trucks on hills without their brakes.
I read those telly pages
And I worry.

Howl

Ride the wolf and see the forest
Flick and fly beside your eye –
See the white frost gleam and glitter
As the winter wolf speeds by.

Ride the wolf – thread your fine fingers
Through the grey hair of his mane.
Touch the roughness, feel the chaffing,
Wonder – will we come again
       To the soft time, to the safe time
       To the time of stout stone walls,
       To the tame time of the fireside,
       To the story-tellers halls?

Ride the wolf and let the moonlight
Sink like silver in your skin.
Breathe the ice blades of the fierce air,
Cut your ties with human kin.
Let the wilderness outside you
Join the wilderness within . . .
The frozen stars will shatter at the shiver of his howl.
No shadow is as subtle or as secret as his prowl.
The grey lord of the winter will not be denied,
So step out of the firelight and

Ride! Ride! Ride!

Otherwise

We took the road to Hippo Loop,
But the land was flooded
And the ground was soup
Just mud and boulder and African clay
So we took another road – went the other way.

We took the road to Baboon Bay
Saw Mamma Warthog and her little ones play.
Tails up high they all ran away
And rolled and rolled in that African clay
So we took another road – went the other way.

We took the road to White Lion Run
And sure enough the big cats come
Their manes hot and bristly like the rays of the sun
They roared their hunger from the African clay
So we took another road – went the other way.

Take another road, take a new road every day,
When you wake up every morning – go another way.
When you wake up every morning – go another way.

A Mean Fish Smile

Sandwich Poets

poems by Roger Stevens, Sue Cowling and Jan Dean

All the very best from three performing poets sandwiched together into one tasty volume.

My Sister is Barmy

My sister is barmy about origami.
She's bats about paper squares.
There are peacocks and chickens
And snakes on her bed.
Blue paper tissue fish
Swim down the stairs.
The ceiling is studded
With frogs, stars and roses,
And three-headed monsters
With long curly noses.
She's folded her homework,
She's folded the post,
One morning at breakfast
She folded the toast!
Really it's wrong to blame origami –
If I'm to be honest, my sister's just barmy.

Jan Dean